# California
# EXAM PREP

CALIFORNIA DEPARTMENT OF REAL ESTATE

Ted Highland, Bobra Tahan,
and Alan Tochterman,
Contributing Editors

This publication is designed to provide accurate and authoritative information in regard to the subject matter covered. It is sold with the understanding that the publisher is not engaged in rendering legal, accounting, or other professional advice. If legal advice or other expert assistance is required, the services of a competent professional should be sought.

President: Dr. Andrew Temte
Chief Learning Officer: Dr. Tim Smaby
Vice President, Real Estate Education: Asha Alsobrooks
Development Editors: Evonna Burr and Kari Domeyer

CALIFORNIA EXAM PREP
© 2010 by Kaplan, Inc.
Published by DF Institute, Inc., d/b/a Kaplan Real Estate Education
332 Front St. S., Suite 501
La Crosse, WI 54601
www.dearbornRE.com

All rights reserved. The text of this publication, or any part thereof, may not be reproduced in any manner whatsoever without written permission from the publisher.

Printed in the United States of America
12 10 9 8 7 6 5 4 3
ISBN: 978-1-4277-2949-1 / 1-4277-2949-2
PPN: 6401-2903

# Contents

Introduction v
Personal Evaluation and Study Guide Worksheet vi
California Real Estate Examination Content vii

**UNIT 1**
## Property Ownership and Land Use Controls and Regulations 1
Classes of Property/Real Estate and Personal Property 2
Property Characteristics 2
Legal Descriptions 2
Types of Ownership—Estates and Encumbrances 3
Types of Ownership 4
Special Categories of Land 4
Government's Rights in Land 5
Zoning 6
Building Codes 7
Environmental Hazards and Regulations 7
Subdivisions 8
Water Rights 9

**UNIT 2**
## Contracts 10
Contract Basics 11
Performance and Discharge of Obligations 11
Essential Elements of a Valid Contract 12
Statute of Frauds 12
Types of Real Estate Contracts 12
Remedies for Breach of Contract/Default 13

**UNIT 3**
## Financing 14
Financing Instruments 15
Foreclosure 16
Methods of Debt Repayment/Debt Service 17
Types of Trust Deeds (and Mortgages) 18
Miscellaneous Mortgage Terms 18
Sources of Capital for Real Estate Loans 19

Government Programs 20
Financing/Credit Laws 21
Loan Brokerage 21

## UNIT 4
# Law of Agency 22
Parties to an Agency Relationship 23
Types of Agency and Creation of Agency 23
Responsibilities of Agent/Disclosure of Agency 24
The Listing Agreement 25
Buyer Agency Agreement 26
Broker/Salesperson Relationships 26

## UNIT 5
# Practice of Real Estate and Mandated Disclosures 28
Fair Housing 29
Trust Accounts and Record Keeping 30
Department of Real Estate (DRE) Disciplinary Actions 30
California Real Estate Recovery Fund 31
Truth in Advertising 32
Mandated Disclosures 32
Property Management/Landlord-Tenant 33

## UNIT 6
# Valuation and Market Analysis 34
Value 35
Methods of Estimating Value/Appraisal Process 36
The Financial Institutions Reform, Recovery, and Enforcement Act (FIRREA) 39

## UNIT 7
# Transfer of Property 40
Alienation 41
Title Insurance 42
Escrow/Settlement/Closing 43
Tax Aspects 44

# Introduction

## ■ KEYS TO SUCCESS

Welcome to **Kaplan Real Estate Education's** Exam Prep review program!

This program contains the most up-to-date information on the state exams for both brokers and salespeople. As you will observe on the following pages (where we provide the California Department of Real Estate's **real estate examination content**), most of the information tested is the same on both the broker and the salesperson exams. Where content is specific to the broker exam, the instructor will point it out for the benefit of broker attendees. Rest assured that you are getting the latest information you need to pass the exam.

At this point, you should have been gaining proficiency using either the agent or the broker version of our **Drill & Practice** series of more than 1,000 sample test questions with detailed explanations. Ideally, before taking the Exam Prep review, you should be attaining scores of 80 percent (85 percent for brokers) or above on these practice questions. Do not attempt to memorize the exact questions and answers. No exam preparation provider has the exact questions and answers found on the state exam. Understanding the concepts is what is important. Successful test-takers have found this to be a key to exam success.

In order to see what level of proficiency you possess before taking the Exam Prep review, we provide you with a **Pre-Test** of 75 questions that mimic the state exam. Complete the Pre-Test and score it. Insert the total number of correct answers in the Pre-Test score box and in each of the individual exam content category boxes in the Personal Evaluation and Study Guide Worksheet on the next page. You can then evaluate where you already have high levels of knowledge and where your weaker areas are so that you can focus your studying immediately before taking your exam. After you take the Exam Prep review, we provide you with a **Post-Test** that you can analyze so you can see the dramatic improvement this class provides.

Key test concepts are reinforced through our unique test-taking approach and teaching methods. Along with the other preparation steps you have already taken, you will now be ready to take and pass the California State Salesperson or Broker License Examination.

Here's to your success!

# Personal Evaluation and Study Guide Worksheet

**Pre-Test Score**

[ ] Passing Score
Sales = 53 questions correct
Broker = 57 questions correct

**Post-Test Score**

[ ] Passing Score
Sales = 53 questions correct
Broker = 57 questions correct

| Exam Content | Pre-Test | | | | | | Post-Test | | | | | |
|---|---|---|---|---|---|---|---|---|---|---|---|---|
| | Your Pre-Test Scores | Very Weak | Weak | Average | Strong | Very Strong | Your Post-Test Scores | Very Weak | Weak | Average | Strong | Very Strong |
| Property Ownership | | 0–6 | 7–8 | 9–10 | 11–12 | 13 | | 0–6 | 7–8 | 9–10 | 11–12 | 13 |
| Laws of Agency | | 0–4 | 5 | 6–7 | 8 | 9 | | 0–4 | 5 | 6–7 | 8 | 9 |
| Valuation and Market Analysis | | 0–4 | 5 | 6–7 | 8 | 9 | | 0–4 | 5 | 6–7 | 8 | 9 |
| Financing | | 0–5 | 6 | 7–8 | 9 | 10 | | 0–5 | 6 | 7–8 | 9 | 10 |
| Transfer of Property | | 0–3 | 4 | 5 | 6 | 7 | | 0–3 | 4 | 5 | 6 | 7 |
| Practice of Real Estate | | 0–9 | 10–11 | 12–14 | 15–16 | 17–18 | | 0–9 | 10–11 | 12–14 | 15–16 | 17–18 |
| Contracts | | 0–4 | 5 | 6–7 | 8 | 9 | | 0–4 | 5 | 6–7 | 8 | 9 |

# California Real Estate Examination Content

## ■ PROPERTY OWNERSHIP AND LAND USE CONTROLS AND REGULATIONS

*Approximately 18 percent of salesperson exam (27 questions)*
*15 percent of broker exam (30 questions)*

- Classes of property
- Property characteristics
- Encumbrances
- Types of ownership
- Descriptions of property
- Government rights in land
- Public controls
- Environmental hazards and regulations
- Private controls
- Water rights
- Special categories of land

## ■ CONTRACTS

*Approximately 12 percent of salesperson exam (18 questions)*
*12 percent of broker exam (24 questions)*

- General
- Listing agreements
- Buyer broker agreements
- Offers/purchase contracts
- Counteroffers/multiple counteroffers
- Leases
- Agreements
- Promissory notes/securities

## ■ FINANCING

*Approximately 13 percent of salesperson exam (20 questions)*
*13 percent of broker exam (26 questions)*

- General concepts
- Types of loans
- Sources of financing
- How to deal with lenders
- Government programs

- Mortgages/deeds of trust/notes
- Financing/credit laws
- Loan brokerage

## LAW OF AGENCY

*Approximately 12 percent of salesperson exam (18 questions)*
*12 percent of broker exam (24 questions)*

- Law, definition and nature of agency relationships, types of agencies, and agents
- Creation of agency and agency agreements
- Responsibilities of agent to seller/buyer as principal
- Disclosure of agency
- Disclosure of acting as principal or other interest
- Termination of agency
- Commission and fees

## PRACTICE OF REAL ESTATE AND MANDATED DISCLOSURES

*Approximately 24 percent of salesperson exam (36 questions)*
*27 percent of broker exam (54 questions)*

- Trust account management
- Fair housing laws
- Truth in advertising
- Record keeping requirements
- Agent supervision
- Permitted activities of unlicensed sales assistants
- DRE jurisdiction and disciplinary actions
- Licensing, continuing education requirements and procedures
- California Real Estate Recovery Fund
- General ethics
- Technology
- Property management/landlord-tenant rights
- Commercial/industrial/income properties
- Specialty areas
- Transfer disclosure statement
- Natural hazard disclosure statements
- Material facts affecting property value
- Need for inspection and obtaining/verifying information

## ■ VALUATION AND MARKET ANALYSIS

*Approximately 12 percent of salesperson exam (18 questions)*
*11 percent of broker exam (17 questions)*

- Value
- Methods of estimating value

## ■ TRANSFER OF PROPERTY

*Approximately 9 percent of salesperson exam (14 questions)*
*10 percent of broker exam (15 questions)*

- Title insurance
- Deeds
- Escrow
- Reports
- Tax aspects
- Special processes

**Note:** You must correctly answer **at least 70 percent** of the 150 questions on the state salesperson exam. You will have 3 hours and 15 minutes to complete the exam.

You must correctly answer **at least 75 percent** of the 200 questions on the state broker exam to pass it. You will have 5 hours to complete the exam. You will have a 2.5-hour session in the morning to complete 100 questions and a 2.5-hour session in the afternoon to complete the remaining 100 questions.

# UNIT 1

# Property Ownership and Land Use Controls and Regulations

(Salesperson 18 percent/27 questions;
Broker 15 percent/30 questions)

## I. CLASSES OF PROPERTY/REAL ESTATE AND PERSONAL PROPERTY

### A. Real estate

Real estate includes land plus improvements plus appurtenances, which include rights, privileges, and fixtures.

1. Land

2. Improvements

### B. Personal property/chattel

1. Everything that is not real estate; _____ items

2. Personal property is transferred by a bill of sale (real property is transferred by deed)

### C. Personal property can become real property and vice versa

1. Personal property becomes real property by attachment.

2. Real property becomes personal property by severance.

## II. PROPERTY CHARACTERISTICS

### A. Physical characteristics of land

1. Immobile—the geographic location of a piece of land is fixed

2. Unique or nonhomogeneous—all parcels differ geographically and each parcel has its own location

### B. Economic characteristics of land

1. Scarcity—although there is a substantial amount of unused land, supply in a given location or of a specific quality can be limited

2. Area preference or situs—people's choices and desires for a given area

## III. LEGAL DESCRIPTIONS

### A. Methods of legal description

1. Metes and bounds—linear measurements, directions, and degrees

2. Rectangular survey/government survey—applies to over 30 states, especially in western United States

3. Recorded map (lot, block, subdivision)—urban/residential

4. Informal reference—street addresses are informal references that are not legal descriptions

Unit 1　Property Ownership and Land Use Controls and Regulations　**3**

### B. Survey

1. Lender may require

2. May reveal encroachments or zoning violations

## IV. TYPES OF OWNERSHIP—ESTATES AND ENCUMBRANCES

Both a tenant renting an apartment building and an owner of a house or condominium have estates in real property.

### A. Freehold estates

1. Fee simple absolute lasts forever and features the maximum control of use.

2. Fee simple defeasible lasts "so long as" the _____ is not broken.

3. Life estate lasts for the duration of a person's lifetime.

### B. Less-than-freehold (leasehold) estates

1. Estate/tenancy for years—predetermined termination date; definite period. No notice is required.

    a) Fixed term

    b) Ends automatically

    c) Advance notice

2. Periodic estate/tenancy—continues from period to period, such as month to month, until proper notice is given. It renews under the same conditions and terms upon payment of rent.

    a) Automatically renews

3. Estate/tenancy at will—continues at owner's consent. California has notice requirements.

4. Estate/tenancy at sufferance—when a "holdover tenant" stays beyond termination without consent. If a landlord accepts payments, it becomes a periodic tenancy.

5. The lessee has a leasehold estate; the lessor holds a leased fee estate and has a reversionary interest.

### C. Encumbrances/imperfections

These are nonpossessory interests in the lands of another. They may create a cloud on the title that might impair or lessen the owner's rights.

1. Easement—nonpossessory right to use the lands of another for a specific purpose

    a) Appurtenant easement

    b) Easement in gross

2. Deed restrictions/restrictive covenants/subdivision deed restrictions/condominium bylaws or CCRs (covenants, conditions, and restrictions)

3. Lien—claim that attaches to and is binding on property to secure debt repayment

4. Encroachment—unauthorized use of another person's land

5. License—revocable permission to use the land of another without creating an estate in land

6. Lis pendens—a recorded document that gives constructive notice of a pending lawsuit

## V. TYPES OF OWNERSHIP

The manner of holding title has significant legal and tax consequences. An attorney specializing in such matters should be consulted. Licensees should NEVER advise on how to take title.

### A. Sole ownership/estate in severalty

1. When property is owned solely and separately by one person or one entity, it is called an _____.

2. A corporation can hold title in severalty.

### B. Concurrent ownership

1. Tenants in common—own undivided fractional shares with no right of survivorship. Each co-owner has _____

2. Joint tenants—co-ownership with the right of survivorship

3. Community property

4. In trust—ownership in a fiduciary capacity for another

5. In partnership

## VI. SPECIAL CATEGORIES OF LAND

### A. Condominium

1. Real estate, portions of which are designated for separate ownership (units) and the remainder of which, _____, is designated for common ownership and use (common elements)

2. Fee simple interest in unit plus undivided interest in common elements as tenants in common transferred by deed

3. Each unit and its common element percentage is taxed, homesteaded, insured, and transferred as a separate parcel

4. Condominium conversion is the process of changing from rental apartments to condominium ownership

## B. Stock cooperative

1. Ownership by a corporation, which in turn leases space to shareholders

2. Buyer receives corporate bylaws, shares of stock, and proprietary lease

3. Since there is no ownership of the unit, the buyer does not receive a deed

4. Owner pays assessments/association fees

## C. Time-shares

1. A common-interest ownership form where multiple owners have interest in a property

2. Each purchaser receives the right to use the facilities for a certain period of time each year

3. Seven-day right of rescission

## D. Planned unit development (PUD)

1. Consists of separately owned parcels of land together with membership in an association which owns common areas (e.g., a gated community)

2. Differs from a condominium in that the property owners actually own the land beneath the house, rather than the air space of the condo unit

Note: Present tenants of a proposed condominium, community apartment project, or stock cooperative must be given notice of the right to purchase their units for 90 days after the issuance of the public report.

## VII. GOVERNMENT'S RIGHTS IN LAND

### A. Collect property taxes and special assessments

1. Ad valorem—according to value

2. May seize and sell by enforcing property tax lien

3. _____ are taxes levied against specific properties that benefit from a public improvement

### B. Eminent domain

1. Right to "take" private land for public use

2. _____ is the process

3. Fair compensation including property value plus damages

### C. Police power

1. Enact and enforce laws governing land use to promote and support the public health, safety, morals, and general welfare

2. Examples include zoning, building codes, subdivision regulations, and safety codes

3. While zoning and so on may affect property value, it is generally not considered a "taking" and requires no compensation

### D. Escheat

1. Government's reversionary right

2. Abandoned property or property of intestate owners with no heirs may revert to the government

## VIII. ZONING

### A. Typical zoning and land use classifications

1. Residential, commercial, industrial/manufacturing, agricultural, mixed

2. Buffer zone is an area of land (e.g., a park) that separates two drastically different land use zones

### B. Typical zoning controls and exceptions

1. Rezoning or amendment is a zoning change for an entire area.

2. Downzoning is a zoning change from dense to less dense usage.

3. Upzoning is a change from less dense to more dense usage.

4. Spot zoning is reclassification of a small area of land for use that does not conform to the zoning of the rest of the area.

5. Legal _____ allows an owner to continue present use that no longer complies with current zoning (also called _____).

6. Setback, sideyard, and rearyard restrictions limit the location of improvements in relation to the position of the street.

7. _____ allows an individual owner to vary or deviate to prevent economic hardship.

8. Special (conditional) use (also called a special exception) is a specific type of variance allowing a different use.

## IX. BUILDING CODES

### A. Regulate building and construction standards

1. Designed to provide minimum standards

2. There are national and local standards— _____

### B. Building inspectors are responsible for enforcing building codes

1. Can make an _____ when safety isn't compromised and standards not specifically violated

## X. ENVIRONMENTAL HAZARDS AND REGULATIONS

### A. Lead-based paint

1. Agent must give copy of U.S. Environmental Protection Agency (EPA) pamphlet to buyers and tenants of homes built _____

2. Buyers have ten-day opportunity to have home tested

3. Include warnings on purchase agreement and obtain signatures of buyers, sellers, and agents

### B. Radon gas

1. An odorless radioactive gas that enters through cracks in the basement and can cause lung cancer

2. EPA has determined what is an action level, but testing is not required

3. Measured in picocuries per liter of air (pCi/L) _____
_____

### C. Asbestos

1. A material used for many years as insulation

2. Asbestos dust can be dangerous or even life threatening

### D. Groundwater contamination

1. Comes from several sources

2. Most common are underground storage tanks, use of pesticides on farms, and waste disposal sites

### E. Environmental impact statement (EIS)

1. A report that assesses the probable impact on the environment of a proposed project

2. Required of federal agencies in advance of major government actions (e.g., new highway or bridge construction)

### F. Superfund law

1. Law involving liability for cleanup of sites affected by toxic materials

2. _____
   _____

## XI. SUBDIVISIONS

### A. Subdivision Map Act

1. Establishes procedures for filing a subdivision plan when property is divided into _____ parcels

2. Controls physical design aspects of a subdivision; ensures that areas devoted to public use, such as streets, will be properly improved initially

### B. Subdivision lands law

1. Describes forms of ownership allowed in a subdivision of _____ parcels

2. Designed to prevent fraud and misrepresentation in selling of subdivisions

3. Public report

### C. Other subdivision requirements

1. An environmental impact report (EIR) is required if a project will have a significant effect on the environment.

2. The Alquist-Priolo Earthquake Fault Zoning Act regulates development in earthquake zones.

3. The Street Improvement Act of 1911 authorizes local governing bodies to order street improvements (off-site improvements) and pay through a bond issue and special assessment.

## XII. WATER RIGHTS

### A. _____

1. Incidental to ownership of land abutting flowing water (stream, river, or _____)

**B.** _____

   1. Incidental to ownership of land abutting water that is not flowing (lake, ocean, or _____)

**C. Other terms**

   1. _____ is the gradual addition to land through natural causes.

   2. *Erosion* is the gradual loss of land through natural causes.

   3. _____ is the sudden loss of land through natural causes.

# Contracts

(Salesperson 12 percent/18 questions;
Broker 12 percent/24 questions)

## I. CONTRACT BASICS

### A. Definition of a contract

1. An agreement between two or more parties to do or not to do a specific thing

### B. Conditions of a contract

1. A _____ contract contains all essential elements.

2. A _____ contract appears to be valid, but one party may disaffirm because, for example, that party was subject to duress, undue influence, fraud, or misrepresentation.

3. A _____ contract is not enforceable due to a failure to contain all essential elements.

### C. Enforceable versus unenforceable

1. In addition to being valid, void, or voidable, a contract can be enforceable or unenforceable.

2. A void contract is, by definition, unenforceable. A voidable contract is enforceable only by the injured party.

3. Valid contracts meet all essential elements but can be _____ by the courts (e.g., certain oral contracts, statute of limitations has expired, laches [not enforced in timely manner]).

### D. Parties to a transaction; -or versus -ee

## II. PERFORMANCE AND DISCHARGE OF OBLIGATIONS

### A. Unilateral versus bilateral

1. Unilateral—promise exchanged for performance

2. Bilateral—promise exchanged for a promise

### B. Executed versus executory

1. Executed—duties completed by both parties; performed

2. Executory—one or both parties need to complete part of the contract; yet to be fully performed

### C. Amendments

1. Changes or modifications to a contract must be in writing and signed by all parties.

### D. Addendum

1. Additional material attached to and made part of the initial agreement document

### E. Statute of limitations

1. Two years for oral contracts
2. Four years for written contracts
3. Doctrine of laches is used by courts to deny a claim because of undue delay in assertion

## III. ESSENTIAL ELEMENTS OF A VALID CONTRACT

- Consent
- Capacity
- Consideration
- Lawful object

## IV. STATUTE OF FRAUDS

### A. Agreement in writing

1. _____ requires that certain contracts be in writing to be enforceable
2. Includes contracts for the transfer of title to real estate but NOT leases of 12 months or less

### B. Agreement signed

1. Both spouses must sign to sell community property or release homestead rights.
2. Only one spouse may sign a listing.

## V. TYPES OF REAL ESTATE CONTRACTS

### A. Purchase agreement/offer to purchase/contract of sale

1. Bilateral/promise for a promise
2. Offer becomes a valid and binding contract when acceptance is communicated
3. Executory until performance by parties (closing)
4. May include contingency clause allowing buyer to terminate under certain conditions
5. A "_____" clause requires performance within time specified
6. Earnest money not required to create valid purchase agreement

## B. Option

1. Owner (optionor) _____ to prospective buyer (optionee) _____

2. Option fee paid by optionee for the right

3. Optionor retains option fee if no performance by optionee

4. Unilateral contract; becomes bilateral when option exercised by optionee

## C. Lease

1. Elements of a lease

2. Lessor gives right to occupy to lessee and has _____ to retake possession

3. Lessee may transfer rights

    a) Sublease

    b) Assignment

4. Types of leases

5. Constructive eviction—a tenant may vacate and be released of all further obligations if lessor does not meet obligations

6. A lease may be terminated by mutual agreement; called a _____

# VI. REMEDIES FOR BREACH OF CONTRACT/DEFAULT

## A. Mutual rescission

1. Mutual cancellation of obligations and return of all parties to their original condition before the contract was executed

## B. Action for damages

1. Suit for monetary damages

2. Accept liquidated damages

## C. Specific performance

1. An action to force another party to buy or sell according to a contract

# Financing

(Salesperson 13 percent/20 questions,
Broker 13 percent/26 questions)

## I. FINANCING INSTRUMENTS

### A. Promissory note

1. Evidence of a debt

2. Secured by mortgage or trust deed

3. A _____ considered personal property; cannot be recorded

### B. Mortgage and deed of trust

1. Security instruments

2. Include covenants—causes of foreclosure

### C. Mortgage

1. A mortgage is a two-party instrument

2. Borrower = mortgagor; lender = mortgagee

3. Most common financing instrument in United States; California, however, favors deed of trust

### D. Deed of trust/trust deed

1. Three-party instrument

2. Borrower = trustor; lender = beneficiary; third party = trustee

3. Property is conveyed by borrower to a third party (trustee) as security for loan

4. Trustee holds naked (bare legal) title on behalf of the lender (beneficiary)

5. Borrower (trustor) holds legal title and deed of trust is a lien

6. Trustee may sell the property in case of default

### E. Satisfaction

1. When a mortgage note is paid, the mortgagee records the satisfaction to release the lien.

2. When a trust note is paid, the trustee records the _____ to release the lien. (Do NOT confuse with a trustee's deed, which is used in the event of foreclosure.)

### F. Assumption versus subject to

1. If a buyer purchases property "subject to" a mortgage, the seller remains liable.

2. If a buyer assumes, the buyer becomes liable for the debt and the lender releases the original borrower's liability.

3. There are no loan origination fees or points when a borrower assumes or purchases subject to a mortgage.

### G. Land contract/real property sales contract/installment contract/contract for deed

1. Form of owner financing and security arrangement

2. Seller (vendor) keeps legal title. Buyer (vendee) has equitable title, takes possession, and makes payments, receiving deed when payments are complete

3. Process used for CalVet loans, where Department of Veterans Affairs (VA) purchases property and sells to veteran under a land contract

4. Vendor _____ use payments from vendee to make any existing loan payments prior to using it for another purpose

## II. FORECLOSURE

Foreclosure is a legal procedure whereby property used as security for a debt is taken by a creditor or sold to pay off the debt.

### A. Judicial foreclosure/equitable action (for mortgages)

1. A lawsuit is brought by a mortgagee in superior court to obtain a court order to sell.

2. The property is sold by the sheriff to the high bidder at a public sale.

3. If the sale proceeds exceed the cost of the sale and foreclosing lien, the excess goes to pay off junior liens in order of priority.

4. _____
_____.

5. If the sale does not cover the loan amount, the lender may file for a _____ _____. But no deficiency judgment can be obtained for purchase-money loans used to finance owner-occupied homes of four units or less.

### B. Trustee's sale (trust deeds)

1. No lawsuit necessary; foreclosure made by public sale

2. Requires three months' notification of default. Within ten days of recording notice of default, copy must be sent to trustor.

3. Notice of sale

4. Property sold to high bidder at trustee's sale. Title transferred under a _____ _____.

5. Deficiency judgments not allowed on nonjudicial foreclosures

### C. Deed in lieu of foreclosure

1. Alternative to foreclosure—mortgagor/trustor deeds to mortgagee/beneficiary

2. Disadvantage to lender—does not wipe out junior liens

## III. METHODS OF DEBT REPAYMENT/DEBT SERVICE

### A. Term (straight)

1. Interest only until maturity at end of term

2. Entire principal in one lump sum

### B. Fully _____

1. Equal payments of principal and interest such that the balance becomes "zero"

2. Interest usually paid in arrears

### C. Partially amortized/balloon

1. Equal payments of principal and interest

2. Balloon before end of term

### D. Graduated payment

1. Lower payments in beginning, payments increase, then level off

2. May have negative amortization (principal may increase)

### E. Adjustable-rate mortgage (ARM)/trust deed

1. Rate subject to change based on changes in an economic index

2. May include interest and/or payment caps

### F. Reverse annuity mortgage/trust deed

1. Payments paid to mortgagor over specific term

2. Due upon sale of property, death of mortgagor(s), or at the end of the term

## IV. TYPES OF TRUST DEEDS (AND MORTGAGES)

A. _____

1. Personal property included as security in addition to real property

2. May be used to finance the purchase of a furnished condominium, etc.

B. _____

1. More than one property is pledged as security.

2. A _____ allows a subdivider to remove individual parcels as they are sold.

C. **Seller carryback purchase money**

1. Owner financing where title transfers to buyer

2. Seller "takes back" a trust deed/mortgage as partial payment; seller has lien

D. **Conventional/insured conventional**

1. Debt repayment is based solely on the borrower's ability to pay; loans are not insured or guaranteed by the government.

2. Depending on the loan-to-value ratio, the lender may require private mortgage insurance (PMI).

3. If required, the PMI premium is paid to Mortgage Guarantee Insurance Corporation (MGIC).

E. _____

1. _____ financing made available in installments as improvements are completed

2. Typically adjustable rate/short term from commercial banks

3. Lender may require a commitment for "take out." A take-out loan replaces the construction loan with longer-term financing

## V. MISCELLANEOUS MORTGAGE TERMS

A. _____/mortgage ratio

1. Maximum percentage of value lender will loan

2. Based on price or appraisal, whichever is less

## B. Equity

1. Market value today
   – Total debt today
   Equity today

2. _____ is the use of debt financing of an investment to maximize the return per dollar of equity invested.

## C. Points/loan origination fee

1. Discount points are charged by the lender _____.

   a) One point = 1 percent of loan amount

2. A loan origination fee is charged by the lender to process and issue a loan.

## D. Other clauses

1. A _____ allows a change in the order/priority of mortgages.

2. A _____ allows a borrower to pay off the loan early, but the lender can charge punitive interest, which is taxed as interest and not cost of sale.

# VI. SOURCES OF CAPITAL FOR REAL ESTATE LOANS

## A. Commercial banks

1. Prefer short-term loans for commercial, business, and new construction

## B. Savings and loan associations

1. Conventional, Federal Housing Administration (FHA), and VA home loans

## C. Mortgage bankers and mortgage brokers

1. Mortgage brokers act as intermediaries between borrowers and lenders but don't usually service loans.

2. Mortgage bankers originate and service loans with deposits and personal money.

## D. Life insurance companies/credit unions/pension funds

1. Prefer long-term commercial and industrial participation loans

2. Lender receives interest plus an equity position in income-producing properties

## VII. GOVERNMENT PROGRAMS

Funds come from qualified lenders approved by the Department of Housing and Urban Development (HUD).

### A. FHA fully insured financing

1. FHA _____ lender against loss due to foreclosure

2. Enables high loan-to-value ratio

3. Mutual mortgage insurance (MMI) premiums may be paid at closing or financed

4. Property must meet _____ (MPRs)

### B. VA fully guaranteed financing

1. _____ lenders against loss on loans to veterans

2. Can have up to 100 percent loan-to-value ratio

3. Two certificates required: Certificate of Eligibility and Certificate of Reasonable Value (CRV)

### C. Miscellaneous aspects of FHA/VA

1. Rules regarding assumption depend on the date of the loan

2. No prepayment penalty

3. Nonveterans may assume VA loans

### D. CalVet (California Veterans Farm and Home Purchase Act)

1. The VA administers the program and is a _____.

2. The VA purchases the property, then resells it to the veteran under a real property sales contract/land contract; the veteran has equitable title and gets legal title when the loan is repaid.

3. The veteran is required to acquire a life insurance policy that will pay off the loan in case of death.

4. Impound accounts (reserves) are also required and there cannot be a prepayment penalty.

### E. The Federal Reserve Bank (The "Fed")

1. The nation's central bank, charged with regulating the nation's money supply

2. Regulates rate of growth/inflation

## F. Secondary mortgage market

1. Where loans are bought and sold; NOT originated

2. Organizations that sell mortgage-backed securities to investors

3. To verify the loan balance upon purchasing the mortgage, the investor or secondary market purchaser will ask for a _____

4. When a loan is sold for less than its face amount, it's called _____

## VIII. FINANCING/CREDIT LAWS

### A. Regulation Z/Truth in Lending—Federal Reserve Board regulates

1. **Purpose:** Promote the informed use of consumer credit by requiring meaningful disclosures about its terms and cost

2. Applies only to loans from institutional lenders to consumers for personal, family, or household purposes

### B. Real Estate Settlement Procedures Act (RESPA)

1. Standardizes closing practices for certain transactions

2. Restricts amount of advance escrow payments for taxes and insurance

3. Lender must give *Guide to Settlement Costs* booklet and good-faith estimate of all closing costs at time of application or within three business days

4. Borrower has _____ Uniform Settlement Statement (HUD-1) _____
_____

5. Prohibits "kickbacks" for unearned fees, such as lenders, insurance agencies, escrow companies, or home protection companies paying money for referrals by brokers

## IX. LOAN BROKERAGE

### A. Mortgage loan disclosure statement

1. Disclosure required for all loans negotiated by licensees for one- to four-family residential transactions

2. Must be signed by both borrower and licensee and delivered to borrower before the borrower becomes obligated

3. Broker lending personal funds must disclose this fact

# Law of Agency

(Salesperson 12 percent/18 questions;
Broker 12 percent/24 questions)

## I. PARTIES TO AN AGENCY RELATIONSHIP

### A. Principal

1. One who employs another to act on his or her behalf

2. Consumer principal is a "client"

### B. Agent/fiduciary

1. One who is employed to represent a principal

2. Fiduciary is the highest trust relationship under law—must put the client's interest above one's own

### C. Third party

1. A party to a transaction who is not a party to the particular agency agreement

2. Consumer third-party buyer is a "customer"

## II. TYPES OF AGENCY AND CREATION OF AGENCY

### A. Types of agency

1. Special agency = Listing agent

2. General agency = Property manager

3. _____ is authorized to perform in place of the principal; accomplished through power of attorney

### B. Creation of agency

1. Express agency is created through an oral or written agreement (before the fact).

2. Agency by ratification is created "after the fact," when a previously unauthorized action is confirmed by a principal.

3. Ostensible agency or _____ is created when a third party is led to believe an agency relationship exists.

4. Compensation is not a requirement of an agency relationship. Who pays the agent does not determine whom the agent represents.

## III. RESPONSIBILITIES OF AGENT/DISCLOSURE OF AGENCY

### A. An agent owes a principal/client _____ obligations (OLD CAR)

1. Obedience
2. Loyalty
3. Disclosure
4. Confidentiality
5. Accounting
6. Reasonable care and skill

### B. Disclosure of representation

1. Representation must be disclosed as soon as practical.
2. An agency disclosure form must be provided and signed before the signing of a listing or writing of an offer.
3. Confirmation of agency relationships is required before entering into a contract.
   (_____)
4. Disclosure if representing or _____ or any person with whom agent has significant relationship (e.g., best friend) is required.
5. If representation changes, a new disclosure is required _____.
6. When representing both the buyer and the seller (dual agency), the agent must get consent of both parties in writing—_____.
7. Brokers owe those they don't represent honesty and fair dealing, _____ _____.

### C. Transfer disclosure statement (TDS)

1. Required of both seller and agent with exceptions, which include foreclosures, co-owner to co-owner sales, or other examples where seller would not have knowledge of the property or would not need disclosure
2. _____ decision requires licensees to disclose what they know and what they _____

### D. Additional disclosures/obligations

(Note: See Practice and Mandated Disclosure Section for further discussion of disclosures)

1. Full fiduciary obligation of disclosure to client

2. Disclosure of material facts to customer

3. Must present all offers. Multiple offers should be presented at the same time

4. Listing agreements generally authorize broker to collect earnest money deposits along with offers. If not authorized to do so, broker can accept deposits, but becomes an agent of the buyer for that deposit

5. Earnest money/deposits

6. Must disclose that commissions are negotiable in listing agreement

### E. Liability for another's acts

1. Each broker is responsible for the professional actions of the salespeople the broker employs.

2. A principal is responsible for misrepresentations made by an agent within the scope of the agent's authority.

### F. Multiple listing service (MLS)

1. MLS is a widely used arrangement in which brokers pool listings and offer "cooperation" to other brokers.

2. Cooperating brokers must obey all the laws of agency.

## IV. THE LISTING AGREEMENT

A listing agreement is a personal service contract/employment contract between a broker and a seller that establishes an agency relationship and grants the broker the authority to seek buyers and obtain offers.

### A. Types of listings

1. Exclusive right to sell

2. Exclusive agency

3. Open/nonexclusive

4. Net listing

5. Option listing

### B. Essential elements of a listing

1. In writing and signed by the owner in order to be enforceable

2. Amount/method of compensation paid to the _____ is negotiable

3. Price and terms

4. _____ beginning and _____ for exclusive listings

5. Agent's authority

### C. How a listing terminates

1. Performance by both parties (_____ of the sale)

2. Expiration of term

3. Revocation by principal/renunciation by broker/mutual rescission

4. Death or incapacity of either broker or seller. (Note: Death of salesperson does not terminate a listing.) _____.

5. Destruction of premises

6. Bankruptcy of either broker or seller

### D. When commissions are earned

1. When broker procures a ready, willing, and able buyer

2. When seller accepts an offer presented by a broker

## V. BUYER AGENCY AGREEMENT

### A. Types of buyer representation agreements

1. An exclusive right to represent authorizes one broker to represent the buyer and requires the buyer to compensate the agent when purchasing property through any source.

## VI. BROKER/SALESPERSON RELATIONSHIPS

### A. Employment contract

1. Regulations of the _____ require brokers to have a written agreement with a salesperson.

2. Under real estate law, salespeople are employees of the broker, even if the contract defines them as independent contractors for tax purposes.

## B. Internal Revenue Service (IRS)

1. IRS may classify a salesperson as an employee or an independent contractor.

2. Employees are under the direct control of their employers and can be told how to perform the job.

3. Independent contractors are compensated based on results; employers have less control over how the job is done.

# UNIT 5

# Practice of Real Estate and Mandated Disclosures

(Salesperson 24 percent/36 questions;
Broker 27 percent/54 questions)

## I. FAIR HOUSING

### A. Civil Rights Act of 1866

1. The Civil Rights Act of 1866 prohibits discrimination based on an individual's race.

### B. Federal fair housing—protected classifications

1. Race (only protected class in the 1866 Civil Rights Act)
2. Religion
3. Color
4. National origin
5. Sex (added in 1974)
6. Family status (added in 1988)
7. Handicap/disability (added in 1988)

### C. California fair housing laws

1. Include the Unruh Civil Rights Act, the Fair Employment and Housing Act (Rumford Act), and the Housing Financial Discrimination Act (Holden Act)
2. Stricter than federal acts; include age and marital status as protected classifications

### D. Prohibited actions

1. Less favorable treatment (including refusal to show property)
2. Discriminatory or restrictive advertising
3. _____—the channeling of potential buyers to or away from particular areas as a means of discrimination
4. _____—also called _____. Inducing people to sell their homes because of the entry into the neighborhood of members of protected classes
5. _____—refusing to offer or limiting loans in certain areas

### E. Americans with Disabilities Act (ADA)

1. Ensures equal _____ to public accommodations for disabled persons
2. Requires removal of architectural and communication barriers when "readily achievable"

3. Allows disabled tenants to make changes at their expense. Owner may require tenant to return property to original condition upon termination of lease

4. Also prohibits employment discrimination against the disabled if more than 15 employees

## II. TRUST ACCOUNTS AND RECORD KEEPING

### A. Trust accounts

1. The purpose of trust fund accounting is to keep a broker's funds separate from the broker's clients.

2. _____ of trust funds with funds belonging to the licensee is prohibited; the actual use of trust funds for purposes other than their intended purpose is conversion and is a felony.

### B. Record keeping

1. Brokers are responsible for maintaining adequate records.

2. Brokers must _____ the trust accounts on a _____ to check that the money in the account is equal to their liability.

3. Trust fund records must be kept for three years and must be open for inspection by the real estate commissioner.

## III. DEPARTMENT OF REAL ESTATE (DRE) DISCIPLINARY ACTIONS

### A. Composition and powers of the DRE

1. The DRE is a department within the Business, Transportation, and Housing Agency and is led by the real estate commissioner.

2. The real estate commissioner is appointed by the governor.

3. Powers of the DRE include regulation of licensees and subdivisions.

4. The DRE does NOT mediate commission disputes or collect penalties from victims of licensees.

### B. Violations of the real estate law—examples of unlawful conduct

1. Knowingly misrepresenting value of property to get a listing or secure a buyer

2. Representing to an owner when seeking a listing that the licensee has obtained a written offer when the licensee has no such written offer

3. Stating or implying that the licensee is prohibited by law or regulation from charging less than the quoted commission

4. Misrepresenting the licensee's relationship with a broker or the broker's responsibility for acts of the licensee

5. Knowingly underestimating closing costs

6. Knowingly making a false or misleading representation regarding the form, amount, and/or treatment of an earnest money deposit

7. Knowingly making a false or misleading representation to a seller financing part of a sale regarding buyer's ability to pay

8. Making an addition or modification to the terms of an agreement previously signed by a party without the knowledge and consent of the party

9. When acting as a principal for real estate paper, making a representation regarding the value of securing property without reasonable basis for believing it is accurate

10. Making a representation regarding the nature and/or condition of the features of a property, the size or boundaries of the property, or the legal use of the property without having a reasonable basis for believing it to be true

11. When acting as an agent, failing to disclose to a prospective purchaser material facts about the property

12. When acting as a listing agent, failing to present any written offer unless instructed by the owner not to present such an offer

13. When acting as a listing agent, presenting competing offers in a manner that would induce the owner to accept an offer that provides greater compensation to the agent

14. Failing to explain to the prospective parties for whom the licensee is acting as an agent the meaning and probable significance of a contingency in an offer or contract that may affect the closing date

15. Failing to disclose to a seller whom the licensee represents the nature and extent of any direct or indirect interest that the licensee expects to acquire as a result of the sale. Also must disclose if a relative or person with whom licensee has a special relationship may be acquiring an interest. Same rule applies to representing a buyer and having an interest in the property buyer may acquire.

16. Failing to disclose to a principal any significant interest the licensee has in an entity the agent recommends

17. When acting as an agent for the seller, refunding any part of an offeror's deposit after the seller has accepted the offer, unless the licensee has express permission from the seller to make the refund

## IV. CALIFORNIA REAL ESTATE RECOVERY FUND

### A. Purpose

1. Portions of license fees are placed into an account from which members of the public can be compensated for illegal acts of licensees.

2. Funds can be disbursed if a judgment has been obtained and the debt is uncollectible from the licensee.

3. The license is _____ until the licensee makes payment back to the fund.

B. _____

1. _____ limit per transaction

2. _____ limit against one licensee

## V. TRUTH IN ADVERTISING

A. **False advertising is grounds for revocation or suspension of a license**

B. **Blind advertising**

1. _____ does not list the name of an agent where an agent is involved.

2. All advertising of an activity for which a license is required must indicate a licensee designation ("agent" would meet the requirement).

## VI. MANDATED DISCLOSURES

A. **Natural hazards disclosure form—sellers and agents must sign**

1. Earthquake disclosures

2. Dam failure inundation

3. Very high fire hazard zone

4. Wildfire risk areas

5. 100-year flood zones

B. **Environmental hazards pamphlet**

1. In addition to disclosing environmental (as opposed to natural) hazards in the TDS, sellers and agents can provide a prepared pamphlet.

2. If pamphlet is provided, neither the seller nor the agent has a duty to provide further information regarding environmental hazards (except for lead-based paint disclosure) unless there is actual knowledge.

C. **Mello-Roos disclosure**

1. The _____ of a one- to four-unit dwelling must disclose if the property is subject to a Mello-Roos lien.

### D. Seller financing disclosure

1. If there is seller financing, the Seller Financing Addendum and Disclosure is required.

### E. Other required disclosures

1. Megan's law—all purchase contracts must include a notice informing buyers or lessees of the public availability of information regarding registered sex offenders

2. Home energy ratings

3. Home inspection notice—for FHA financing or HUD-owned property, borrower must sign notice ("Importance of a Home Inspection")

4. Smoke detector notice

5. Water heater bracing

## VII. PROPERTY MANAGEMENT/LANDLORD-TENANT

### A. License requirement

1. A real estate license is required for property managers who rent, lease, solicit listings of places for rent, solicit for prospective tenants, and collect rents.

2. A license is not required for a resident manager, if management activities are confined to the complex in which the manager lives.

### B. Security deposits

1. Amount of security deposits that can be collected depends on specific facts

### C. Landlord warrants

1. Warranty of quiet enjoyment—lease will not be disturbed by someone claiming paramount title

2. Warrant of habitability—landlord must keep property in livable condition

3. If these are violated, tenant may have right of _____

### D. Unlawful detainer

1. A court action by a lessor to regain possession (eviction)

2. Notice to quit required

# Valuation and Market Analysis

(Salesperson 12 percent/18 questions;
Broker 11 percent/17 questions)

Unit 6  Valuation and Market Analysis  **35**

## I. VALUE

An appraisal is an _____ supported by an analysis of relevant property data.

### A. Market value

Market value is the highest price in terms of cash or its equivalent that a property will bring when

1. a willing seller would sell and a willing buyer would buy,
2. the property is exposed for a reasonable time,
3. both parties are familiar with the property's uses, and
4. neither is under abnormal pressure to sell or buy.

### B. Market price

1. The actual price paid in a transaction; price may deviate from value

### C. Essential elements of value (DUST)—cost is NOT an element of value

1. **D**emand
2. **U**tility
3. **S**carcity
4. **T**ransferability

### D. Forces influencing value

1. Physical
2. Economic
3. Governmental
4. Social

### E. Subjective versus objective value

1. Subjective value—value in use
2. Objective value—_____

### F. Principles of value

1. Highest and best use

2. Principle of substitution

3. Supply and demand

4. Anticipation—value can increase or decrease due to some future benefit or detriment that will affect the property

5. Conformity

6. Regression—value of overimproved property declines

7. Progression—value of underimproved property increases

8. Plottage—the increased value resulting from _____ (act), combining adjacent lots into one larger lot

9. Balance—point of maximum productivity and maximum value is achieved when all factors of production (land, labor, capital, and coordination) are in balance

10. Contribution—the value of an improvement depends upon how much it adds or detracts from the overall value

## II. METHODS OF ESTIMATING VALUE/APPRAISAL PROCESS

### A. Sales comparison approach/market approach/market data approach—primarily residential

1. Property evaluating—"subject"

2. Similar properties recently sold—"comparables" or "comps"

3. Adjustments made to comparables

4. Comp better "–", comp worse "+"

5. _____ (CMA) uses similar approach but is not an appraisal

6. Whenever possible, property evaluated using comparison with recent sales

### B. Cost approach/replacement cost approach—most effective method for special purpose buildings or new construction

1. Estimate new construction cost

2. Reproduction cost new—exact replica

3. Replacement cost new—same function or utility

4. Methods of estimating cost of new construction

   a) _____ is a highly involved process of estimating cost of new construction by detailing raw material and installation costs; most difficult but most accurate method (rarely used)

   b) _____ method estimates the installed price of components

   c) _____ method estimates cost based on the dimensions of the property (most commonly used)

   d) _____ method (least accurate)

| Physical Deterioration | Functional Obsolescence | Economic Obsolescence |
|---|---|---|
| Internal (inside the property lines) | Internal (inside the property lines) | External (outside the property lines) |
| Loss of value (dollar amount) associated with wear and tear | Loss of value (dollar amount) associated with design, layout, etc. | Loss of value (dollar amount) associated with forces outside the property lines |
| Curable<br>Incurable | Curable<br>Incurable | Incurable |

5. Estimate and add in land value (using market approach)

6. Economic life = theoretical life

   a) Period of time from date of construction that the improvement will add value to the land

   b) Frame house: 40–60 years

7. Effective age = how old the improvement appears to be

8. Actual or chronological age = how old it really is

9. Remaining economic life = period of time from date of appraisal that the improvement will continue to add value to the land

10. Formula:

    a) Economic life – Effective age = Remaining economic life

    b) Remaining economic life = Economic life – Effective age

## C. Income approach—income-producing properties

1. Capitalization

2. Income = Rate × (times) Value

   I = Net annual income, R = Cap rate, V = Value

   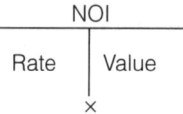

3. Potential gross income

   a) Contract (scheduled) rent

   b) Market rent

   − Vacancy and collection losses (percent of potential gross)
   Effective gross income
   − Operating expenses (do not include debt service)
   Net operating income (NOI)

   $$\frac{NOI}{Capitalization\ rate} = Value$$

4. Gross rent multiplier (alternative to capitalization that takes into account _____ but not expenses)

   Formulas:

   Annual gross rent multiplier × Annual gross rent = Value

   OR

   Monthly gross rent multiplier × Monthly gross rent = Value

## D. Additional techniques/variations

1. Development method—vacant land

2. Property residual technique is used in the income approach to estimate the total value of the property, including land and improvements

## E. Frontage/front foot/4-3-2-1 rule

1. _____ is the length of the property abutting a street.

2. Front foot is a measure of frontage used in appraising value of commercial property; each front foot is presumed to extend the depth of the lot.

3. 4-3-2-1 rule is used for commercial property.

### F. Reconciliation process

1. Final step in valuation process: Appraiser analyzes and weighs estimates of value from market, cost, and income approaches

2. Arrives at final estimate of value; NOT an average of the value estimates

### G. A _____ is the most comprehensive type of appraisal report

## III. THE FINANCIAL INSTITUTIONS REFORM, RECOVERY, AND ENFORCEMENT ACT (FIRREA)

### A. Appraisers must comply with Uniform Standards of Professional Appraisal Practice (USPAP)

### B. California licensing requirements

1. An appraiser with a _____ may appraise residential property (one to four units) up to a transaction value of $1 million.

2. An appraiser who is a _____ appraiser may appraise all residential and nonresidential property up to a transaction value of $250,000.

3. An appraiser who is a _____ appraiser may perform all appraisals.

# UNIT 7

# Transfer of Property

(Salesperson 9 percent/14 questions;
Broker 10 percent/15 questions)

## I. ALIENATION

### A. Alienating property

1. *Alienating property* means conveying property—the opposite of acquisition

2. Can be voluntary or involuntary

### B. Types of deeds

Every deed conveys whatever interest is held by the grantor, unless it specifically states that it is conveying a lesser interest. The major difference between types of deeds lies in the extent of the promises given by the grantor to the grantee.

1. Grant deed—most common

2. Quitclaim deed

3. Warranty deed—has five covenants and a guarantee of title (seldom used in California because of prevalence of title insurance)

4. Gift deed—given in return for "love and affection"

5. Involuntary deeds—must be recorded to be effective

### C. Essential elements of a valid deed

1. In writing

2. Signed by _____

3. Competent grantor

4. Granting clause (words of conveyance)

5. Adequate description of property

6. Must designate a grantee

Not required: Date, signature of grantee, and legal description

### D. Essentials for a valid transfer

1. Valid deed

2. Delivered—must pass out of control of grantor during grantor's lifetime; controlled by the intention of the grantor to convey property

3. Accepted by grantee(s)—evidenced by possession of deed, encumbering title, or any act demonstrating ownership, such as taking possession

### E. Conveyance after death

1. *Probate* is the judicial process to prove or confirm validity of a will, collect assets, pay debts and taxes, and distribute all of a deceased's assets.

2. *Devise* is the act of transferring a deceased's (called the devisor or testator) interest in real estate to another (devisee) by will.

3. If intestate, laws of descent and intestate succession determine heirs/descendents.

4. _____ if a property is sold through probate.

### F. Involuntary alienation

1. _____ is ownership granted by the courts due to actual, open, continuous, hostile, notorious, and exclusive possession of another's land for five years under claim of right or color of title. Taxes must be paid for five years.

2. _____ is an easement gained through adverse possession. _____ _____.

3. *Easement by necessity* is an easement created by law to prevent landlocked property. The grantee receives an easement over the grantor's land but only if there is no other access to the grantee's land.

### G. Public transfer

1. The state transfers ownership to a private party by land patent or _____.

2. A conveyance of property from a private party to the state is a _____.

### H. Recording

1. Generally not required for validity (although involuntary transfers require recording to be effective)

2. Gives constructive (legal) notice to protect interests (taking possession also gives constructive notice)

3. Can determine priority (first in time, without notice is first in right)

4. Record in the county where property is located

## II. TITLE INSURANCE

### A. Buyer's goal is to obtain marketable (merchantable) title

## B. Title insurance

1. Examiner checks abstract of title for history of conveyances and traces the chain of title.

2. _____ lists current title status and encumbrances, and certifies that the records are accurate as recorded.

3. A preliminary report is an offer to issue a policy based on the conditions of the report.

4. Types of policies are the following:

    a) Standard (CLTA)

    b) Extended policy (ALTA)

5. _____.

6. Premium is paid once, at the time the policy is issued.

## III. ESCROW/SETTLEMENT/CLOSING

### A. Escrow/settlement procedures

1. *Escrow* or *settlement* is the means by which parties to a contract carry out the terms of an agreement.

2. Parties appoint a third party to act as an escrow agent, usually a title company.

3. The seller's deed and the buyer's money are deposited with an escrow agent according to an escrow agreement that sets forth conditions to be met before the sale will be consummated.

4. Once in escrow, funds can be released upon written instructions of _____ (mutual release papers), through court action (_____), or through a _____ decision.

5. If the purchase agreement and the escrow instructions disagree, _____ _____ because they would be the later contract.

6. During escrow, the escrow agent is a dual agent, representing both parties in the transaction. Once the transaction closes, the escrow agent may become the _____ _____ for any remaining issues pertaining to the parties.

7. The escrow agent collects reports required for the transaction.

8. A "complete escrow" is where all instructions have been completed but the transaction has not yet closed.

### B. Closing statement—debits and credits

1. *Credit to seller* is anything that increases the amount of money the seller takes from the closing. Example: Sale price, prepaid taxes

2. *Debit to seller* is anything that decreases the amount of money the seller takes from the closing. Example: Brokerage fee, mortgage payoff

3. *Credit to buyer* is anything that decreases the amount of money the buyer must bring to the closing. Example: Earnest money, new mortgage

4. *Debit to buyer* is anything that increases the amount of money the buyer must bring to the closing. Example: _____, discount points (if paid by buyer)

5. Proration is based on a 360-day year (30-day months). Rent is paid in advance; mortgage interest is paid in arrears.

6. Insurance may be _____—when the policy is cancelled prior to its expiration.

## IV. TAX ASPECTS

### A. Property taxes—"at value"—"ad valorem"

1. The assessment roll establishes the tax base.

2. Properties can be reassessed for current value and improvements. Reassessments can be appealed to an assessor's appeals board.

3. Fiscal year for property taxes begins on July 1. (See Figure 7.1.)

    a) The first installment, covering July 1 to December 31, is due November 1.

    b) The second installment, covering January 1 to June 30, is due February 1.

**FIGURE 7.1**

**Fiscal tax calendar**

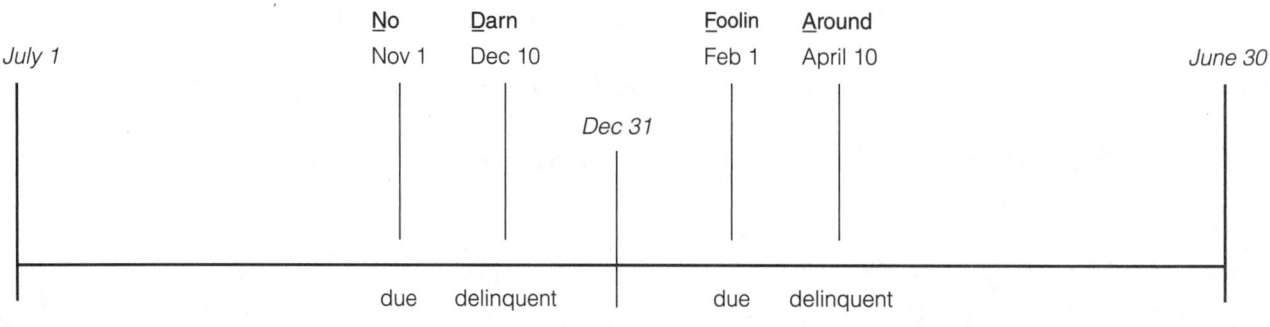

## B. Special assessments

1. Taxes charged against specific properties that benefit from a public improvement

2. Paid along with property taxes and enforced by a lien

## C. Mello-Roos Community Facilities Act of 1982

1. Created a special form of property assessment involving an improvement bond; does not appear on property tax bill

2. _____ of a one- to four-unit dwelling must disclose if property is subject to a Mello-Roos lien

## D. Documentary transfer tax

1. City or county tax rate of .55 per $500 or _____ of purchase price minus existing loans transferred

## E. Depreciation

1. For tax purposes, non-owner-occupied residential properties can be depreciated over 27½ years.

2. Nonresidential (commercial, industrial) properties can be depreciated over 39 years.

3. Only improvements are depreciated—never land.

## F. Capital gains exemption for principal residence

1. No tax on the first $250,000 of profit (single) or $500,000 of profit (married) from the sale of principal residence

2. Must reside in residence two out of the last five years

3. Exemption can be taken every two years (once in a lifetime limit no longer exists)

## G. _____

1. The purchaser of a business may have successor's liability if the sales taxes have not been fully paid by the seller.

2. The purchaser should get a certificate of clearance from the _____ showing that the seller has paid all sales taxes due.

## H. Tax shelters

1. Associated with _____

# Notes